DISASTER ZONE
TORNADOES

by Cari Meister

Ideas for Parents and Teachers

Pogo Books let children practice reading informational text while introducing them to nonfiction features such as headings, labels, sidebars, maps, and diagrams, as well as a table of contents, glossary, and index.

Carefully leveled text with a strong photo match offers early fluent readers the support they need to succeed.

Before Reading

- "Walk" through the book and point out the various nonfiction features. Ask the student what purpose each feature serves.
- Look at the glossary together. Read and discuss the words.

Read the Book

- Have the child read the book independently.
- Invite him or her to list questions that arise from reading.

After Reading

- Discuss the child's questions. Talk about how he or she might find answers to those questions.
- Prompt the child to think more. Ask: Have you ever been in a tornado? What would you do if your school were in the path of a tornado?

Pogo Books are published by Jump!
5357 Penn Avenue South
Minneapolis, MN 55419
www.jumplibrary.com

Library of Congress Cataloging-in-Publication Data

Meister, Cari, author.
   Tornadoes / by Cari Meister.
      pages cm. – (Disaster zone)
   Audience: Ages 7-10.
   Includes bibliographical references and index.
   ISBN 978-1-62031-225-4 (hardcover: alk. paper) –
   ISBN 978-1-62031-268-1 (paperback) –
   ISBN 978-1-62496-312-4 (ebook)
   1. Tornadoes–Juvenile literature. I. Title.
   QC955.2.M454 2016
   551.55'3–dc23

                                    2014044197

Series Editor: Jenny Fretland VanVoorst
Series Designer: Anna Peterson
Photo Researcher: Anna Peterson

Photo Credits: All photos by Shutterstock except:
Alamy, 4, 12-13; Corbis, 18; Getty, 19, 20-21, 23;
National Geographic, 14-15; Thinkstock, 10-11.

Printed in the United States of America at
Corporate Graphics in North Mankato, Minnesota.

TABLE OF CONTENTS

DANGER

CHAPTER 1

IT'S A TORNADO!

Imagine you are visiting your aunt in Oklahoma. The air is hot and sticky. The sky looks green. Soon you hear thunder.

A **funnel cloud** dips from a storm cloud. It starts to swirl and twist. It's a tornado!

funnel cloud · · · · · ▶

Sirens sound.

You and your aunt take cover in the basement. The tornado whips and whirls. It uproots trees. It tosses cars across the road.

After a few minutes it grows quiet.

The radio announcer says it is safe to come out. You go upstairs. The roof is gone. **Debris** is everywhere. But you are safe.

You just survived a tornado.

debris

Tornados are spinning **columns** of air. They form when wet, warm winds meet dry, cold winds. When the winds meet, the warm air rises above the cold air. As it rises, it cools and falls. It starts to spin. The whirling winds form a funnel. If it touches the ground, it becomes a tornado.

TAKE A LOOK!

Tornadoes form when hot and cold winds meet.

■ = cold air
■ = hot air

funnel

strong winds

cloud of debris

CHAPTER 2

· ·

MEASURING AND MAPPING

Some tornados are small. They might be just a few feet (1 meter) across. Others are huge. They can be more than a mile (1.6 kilometers) across.

Experts measure tornados by their wind speed and the damage they cause. Some tornadoes have had winds of more than 300 miles per hour (483 kph)!

Tornadoes have touched down on every continent but Antarctica. The United States has about 1,200 of them each year. They mostly occur in an area known as **Tornado Alley**. They are most common in late spring and early fall.

WHERE ARE THEY?

Tornado Alley covers much of the **Great Plains**, between the Rocky Mountains and the Mississippi River.

UNITED STATES

N
W — E
S

■ = Tornado Alley

When tornadoes happen over water, they form **waterspouts**. They can wreck boats. They can put lives in danger.

There are more waterspouts off the Florida coast than anywhere else in the world.

DID YOU KNOW?

Waterspouts can form over lakes. In 2003, a record number formed over the **Great Lakes**. More than 65 were seen!

waterspout ·····▶

CHAPTER 3

DEADLY TORNADOES

The United States has more tornadoes than any other country in the world. But it is not the site of the deadliest tornado.

On April 26, 1989, a tornado hit Bangladesh in Southeast Asia. It killed more than 1,300 people and injured 12,000. Up to 80,000 people were left homeless.

If there is a threat of a tornado, go to the lowest floor in your home. Stay away from windows. Cover your head. Make sure you are wearing shoes.

Keep a flashlight, a cell phone, and a radio nearby. If you are outside, lie flat in a **ditch**.

Disasters can happen anytime. But be prepared, and you can survive a tornado.

ACTIVITIES & TOOLS

TORNADO IN A BOTTLE

By spinning the bottle in a circular motion, you create a whirlpool that looks like a mini tornado.

What You Need:
- a clear, leak-proof bottle with a cap
- dishwashing soap
- glitter
- water

1. Fill the bottle ¾ full with water.
2. Add three drops of dishwashing liquid.
3. Add some glitter. This will help you see the tornado better.
4. Put the cap on.
5. Hold the bottle upside down by its neck.
6. Spin the bottle quickly in a circular motion for a few seconds and then stop.
7. Do you see a mini tornado? If not, try spinning it again.

GLOSSARY

column: A shape that is tall and thin.

debris: Pieces that are left behind after something has been destroyed.

ditch: A long, narrow hole dug near a road or field.

funnel cloud: A cloud that is shaped like a cone, with a tube coming down from its point.

Great Lakes: Five large lakes near the border of Canada and the United States; they are Lake Huron, Lake Erie, Lake Superior, Lake Michigan, and Lake Ontario.

Great Plains: A large area of flat grassland in the United States that lies between the Mississippi River and the Rocky Mountains.

Tornado Alley: A term used to describe the place where tornadoes most often occur in the United States.

waterspout: An intense, spinning column of wind and water that forms over water.

INDEX

TO LEARN MORE

Learning more is as easy as 1, 2, 3.

1) Go to www.factsurfer.com

2) Enter "tornadoes" into the search box.

3) Click the "Surf" to see a list of websites.

With factsurfer, finding more information is just a click away.